First episode psychosis

An information guide

Sarah Bromley, OT Reg (Ont)

Monica Choi, MD, FRCPC

Sabiha Faruqui, MSc (OT)

camh

Centre for Addiction and Mental Health

A Pan American Health Organization /
World Health Organization Collaborating Centre

Library and Archives Canada Cataloguing in Publication

Bromley, Sarah, 1969-, author
    First episode psychosis : an information guide : a guide for people with
psychosis and their families / Sarah Bromley, OT Reg (Ont), Monica Choi,
MD, Sabiha Faruqui, MSc (OT). -- Revised edition.

Revised edition of: First episode psychosis / Donna Czuchta, Kathryn
    Ryan. 1999.
Includes bibliographical references.
Issued in print and electronic formats.
ISBN 978-1-77052-595-5 (PRINT).--ISBN 978-1-77052-596-2 (PDF).--
ISBN 978-1-77052-597-9 (HTML).--ISBN 978-1-77052-598-6 (ePUB).--
ISBN 978-1-77114-224-3 (Kindle)

    1. Psychoses--Popular works. I. Choi, Monica Arrina, 1978-, author
II. Faruqui, Sabiha, 1983-, author III. Centre for Addiction and Mental
Health, issuing body IV. Title.

RC512.B76 2015   616.89   C2015-901241-4
                                                    C2015-901242-2

Printed in Canada

This publication may be available in other formats. For information about alterna-
tive formats or other CAMH publications, or to place an order, please contact
CAMH Publications:
Toll-free: 1 800 661-1111
Toronto: 416 595-6059
E-mail: publications@camh.ca
Online store: http://store.camh.ca
Website: www.camh.ca

Disponible en français sous le titre :
*Le premier épisode psychotique : Guide pour les personnes atteintes de psychose et leur
famille*

This guide was produced by CAMH Publications.

3973h / 04-2015 / PM115-EN

Contents

Acknowledgments

We acknowledge and thank the following individuals for their support and contributions to this revised edition:

Dr. Ofer Agid, MD
Dr. Crystal Baluyut, MD, FRCPC
Yarissa Herman, DPsych, CPsych
Mary-Lynn Porto, MSW, MHSc, CHE

We also acknowledge Donna Romano, RN, MSc, and Kathryn Ryan, RN, MSc(N), the authors of the original edition; and Jean Addington, PhD, who updated the guide in 2007.

Finally, we extend our thanks to the patients and families of the First Episode Psychosis Program who assisted us with the initial edition of this guide.

Introduction

The purpose of this information guide is to provide information about a first episode of psychosis, its treatment and recovery. It has been written for people experiencing a first episode of psychosis and their family members, to help them gain a better understanding of this illness. Increased awareness of the signs and symptoms of psychosis promotes early detection and appropriate treatment and, in turn, more successful recovery from the psychotic episode.

Early intervention for people experiencing psychosis has many benefits, including:
· reduced secondary problems, such as disruption of work, school and relationships
· retention of social skills and support
· less need for hospitalization
· more rapid recovery and better prognosis
· reduced family disruption and distress
· less resistance to treatment and lower risk of relapse.

1 What is psychosis?

The word psychosis is used to describe conditions that affect the mind, in which people have trouble distinguishing between what is real and what is not. When this occurs, it is called a psychotic episode.

Psychosis usually first appears in a person's late teens or early twenties. Approximately three out of 100 people will experience an episode of psychosis in their lifetime. Psychosis affects men and women equally and occurs across all cultures and socioeconomic groups.

What is a first episode of psychosis?

A first episode of psychosis is the first time a person experiences a psychotic episode. A first episode of psychosis is often very frightening, confusing and distressing, particularly because it is an unfamiliar experience. Unfortunately, there are also many negative stereotypes and misconceptions associated with psychosis that can further add to one's distress.

Psychosis is treatable. Many people recover from a first episode of psychosis and never experience another psychotic episode.

2 The symptoms of psychosis

Psychosis affects the way a person thinks, feels and behaves. The experience of psychosis varies greatly from person to person. Psychosis can come on suddenly or can develop very gradually.

The symptoms of psychosis are often categorized as either "positive" or "negative." People may also experience some cognitive and other symptoms.

Positive symptoms

Positive symptoms are those that *add to or distort* the person's normal functioning. They include:

DELUSIONS

Delusions are false beliefs that are firmly held and are out of keeping with the person's cultural environment. A person may be truly convinced of a belief that is not shared by others, and even the most logical argument cannot change his or her mind. Some common delusions include beliefs of:
· being followed by others
· being monitored by cameras

- having special abilities or powers
- certain songs or comments communicating a hidden message
- one's thoughts being controlled by an outside force.

HALLUCINATIONS

During psychosis, people may hear, see, smell, taste or feel something that is not actually there. For example, they may hear voices or noises that no one else hears, see things that are not there, or experience unusual physical sensations. These changes in perception are called hallucinations.

DISORGANIZED SPEECH, THOUGHTS OR BEHAVIOUR

Disorganized speech might involve a person switching rapidly from one subject to the next, or being so garbled that speech is not comprehensible.

People experiencing psychosis may have changes in their thinking patterns and may find it hard to concentrate and follow a conversation. Their thoughts may speed up, slow down or become jumbled, or they may not connect in a way that makes sense.

Behaviour also may be disorganized. For example, the person may have difficulties performing regular activities of daily living, such as cooking or self-care. Or they may display inappropriate behaviours or affect, such as laughing while talking about a tragic event.

Negative symptoms

Negative symptoms involve normal functioning becoming lost or reduced. These symptoms are often not as obvious as positive symptoms. They may include:
- restricted emotional and facial expression
- restricted speech and verbal fluency
- difficulty with generating ideas or thoughts
- reduced ability to begin tasks
- reduced socialization and motivation.

Other symptoms

Other symptoms or difficulties often occur alongside the psychotic symptoms. They include:
- cognitive symptoms, such as difficulties with attention, concentration, memory and executive function (e.g., planning and organizing, sequencing and behavioural inhibition)
- mood changes—the person may be unusually excited, depressed or anxious, or have highly changeable moods
- suicidal thoughts or behaviours
- substance abuse
- sleep disturbances
- difficulties in functioning.

Some people experiencing a psychotic episode may feel very depressed, and think that life is not worth living. People experiencing suicidal thoughts may attempt to hurt themselves. Suicidal thoughts should always be discussed with a health professional/therapist. Family members may need support and assistance to cope effectively in such situations.

3 Phases of psychosis

Psychosis has three phases. However, not all people who experience a psychotic episode will experience clear symptoms of all three phases—each person's experience will differ.

Prodromal phase

The prodromal phase usually lasts several months, though the duration can vary. This first phase of psychosis involves symptoms that may not be obvious, such as changes in feelings, thoughts, perceptions and behaviours.

Some common prodromal symptoms are:
· reduced concentration and attention, disorganized thoughts
· reduced motivation, changes in energy level, less interest in usual activities
· social withdrawal
· sleep disturbance
· suspiciousness
· irritability, anxiety, depressed mood
· no longer going to school or work, or performance deteriorating
· intense focus on particular ideas, which may seem odd or disturbing to others.

These symptoms are very general, and may not necessarily be a sign of psychosis. For example, they could represent normal adolescent behaviour. Family members should track these changes over time—if they persist, this may suggest a prodromal phase.

Acute phase

In the acute, or active, phase, people typically experience positive psychotic symptoms, such as hallucinations, delusions and disorganized thinking. Some negative symptoms may also emerge. This phase is the easiest to recognize and diagnose, and so it is when most people begin receiving treatment. The earlier treatment starts, the greater the chance of successful recovery.

Recovery phase

In the recovery, or residual, phase, acute symptoms reduce in intensity, though some may not disappear altogether. After recovery from a first episode of psychosis, some people never experience a relapse (a second episode). To reduce the risk of relapse, it is very important to continue medication and other treatments as recommended by the physician and clinical team.

The recovery process—how long it takes and how much improvement there is—varies from person to person. Once the acute symptoms of psychosis have responded to treatment, help may still be needed with issues such as depression, anxiety, decreased self esteem, social problems and school or work difficulties.

In addition, family members may need help and support to cope effectively. In urgent situations, such as those involving potential harm to the person experiencing psychosis, the person should be taken to the emergency department of the closest hospital to receive treatment.

Symptoms of psychosis get better with treatment.

4 The causes of psychosis

Psychosis occurs in a variety of mental and physical disorders, so it is often difficult to know what has caused a first episode. Research shows that a combination of biological factors, including genetic factors, create a situation where a person is vulnerable to (at a greater risk of) developing psychotic symptoms. For such a person, a psychotic episode may be triggered by many different environmental factors, such as stressful events or substance use. These factors are discussed below.

An imbalance in certain neurotransmitters (brain chemicals), including dopamine and serotonin, can also be a factor in the development of psychosis.

Stress and psychosis

Potential sources of life stress that may play a role in triggering an episode of psychosis include:
· physical stress, such as irregular sleep, binge drinking, use of street drugs, poor routine, poor diet, physical sickness
· environmental stress, such as inadequate housing, lack of social support, unemployment, major life changes (e.g., starting a new school or job)

- emotional stress, such as relationship problems, difficulties with family or friends
- acute life events, such as bereavement, accidents, illness, trouble with the law, pregnancy or childbirth, physical or sexual assault or abuse
- chronic stress, such as trouble with housing, or money
- bullying, such as racism or homophobia, cyber-bullying.

One way of thinking about the effect of stress is through the image of a "stress bucket" (Brabben & Turkington, 2002). In a person with a biological vulnerability to psychosis, accumulated stress can cause his or her stress bucket to eventually overflow. This overflow increases the risk that psychosis may develop.

Substance use and psychosis

Some drugs, such as amphetamines, can directly induce psychosis. Others, including cannabis (marijuana), can cause a psychotic episode by increasing a person's existing vulnerability to psychosis. There is also the risk that a psychotic episode in the context of substance use may cause the onset of a chronic (long-term) psychotic disorder.

CANNABIS AND PSYCHOSIS

Several decades ago, cannabis was considered a "soft" drug. Today, however, it is better understood that cannabis use can increase the risk of developing psychosis. The earlier someone starts using cannabis, and the more they use, the higher their risk of developing psychosis later in life.

Cannabis use increases the risk of a person developing schizophrenia, whether or not other risk factors such as genetics and stress are present. In addition, ongoing cannabis use makes the symptoms of psychosis less responsive to treatment and increases the risk of relapse (recurrence of the symptoms).

5 The different types of psychosis

There are a number of mental illnesses that can include psychosis as a symptom. In the early phases of a psychotic episode, it is usually difficult to diagnose the exact type of psychotic disorder that is happening. This is because the factors that determine a specific diagnosis are often unclear during the psychotic episode. It is important to recognize and understand symptoms, and to communicate them to the treatment team. Any concerns or questions about diagnosis should be discussed with a mental health professional. A thorough medical assessment, to rule out any physical illness that may be the cause of the psychosis, may be indicated.

The following list provides the names and brief descriptions of different types of psychotic illness.

Schizophrenia

The term schizophrenia refers to a diagnosis in which a person experiences some psychotic symptoms for at least six months, with a significant decline in the person's ability to function. The symptoms and length of the illness vary from person to person.

Schizophreniform disorder

This type of psychosis is the same as schizophrenia except that the symptoms have lasted for at least one month and no more than six months. The illness may completely resolve or may persist and progress to other psychiatric diagnoses, such as schizophrenia, bipolar disorder or schizoaffective disorder.

Bipolar disorder

With this type of illness the symptoms of psychosis relate more to mood disturbance than to a thought disturbance. A person will experience elevated mood (mania) and sometimes depression, which may persist or fluctuate in intensity. When psychotic symptoms arise, they often reflect the person's mood. For example, people who are depressed may hear voices that put them down. People who are experiencing an elevated mood may believe they are special and are capable of doing amazing things.

Schizoaffective disorder

During this type of psychosis, a person will experience symptoms of schizophrenia and at, some point in the course of illness, concurrent symptoms of a mood disturbance.

Depression with psychotic features

Sometimes a person will experience a severe depression with symptoms of psychosis, without the mania associated with bipolar disorder. This type of depression is referred to as a psychotic depression or depression with psychotic features.

Drug-induced psychosis

The use of drugs such as marijuana, cocaine, ecstasy, ketamine, LSD, amphetamines and alcohol can sometimes cause psychotic symptoms to appear. In drug-induced psychosis, once the effects of the drugs wear off, the symptoms of psychosis can spontaneously resolve or may require medical treatment.

Organic psychosis

Symptoms of psychosis may appear as a result of a physical illness or a head injury. A thorough medical examination should be conducted to rule out or confirm this type of psychosis. This examination may involve some tests or investigations such as a brain scan.

Brief psychotic disorder

Sometimes symptoms of psychosis come on suddenly and, in some cases, are triggered by a major stress in the person's life, such as a death in the family. This type of psychosis lasts less than a month.

Delusional disorder

This type of psychosis consists of very strong and fixed beliefs in things that are not true. Changes in perception, such as hallucinations, are not seen in this illness. A delusional disorder does not usually affect a person's ability to function.

It may be difficult to make a diagnosis in the early stages of psychosis. Often patterns of symptoms must be assessed over many months, and determining a diagnosis may take some time. Therefore, initially it may be more helpful to focus on the symptoms and their impact on the person's functioning rather than on a particular diagnosis. It is also important to remember that everyone's experience of psychosis is different: the course and the outcome will vary from person to person.

6 Treatment of psychosis

Psychosis can be treated, and many people make a good recovery. Research suggests that the earlier intervention can occur, the better the treatment outcome. Therefore, it is important to get help as early as possible. However, in the early stages of psychosis, people often do not know what is happening to them, and do not seek treatment right away. Some people may feel there is nothing wrong or that symptoms will go away on their own. Others, if they are aware of the problem, may have concerns about the required treatment.

Assessment

Before a specific treatment is recommended, a thorough assessment is completed by mental health professionals, a group that can include psychiatrists, psychologists, psychiatric nurses, occupational therapists and social workers. Part of the evaluation is a comprehensive interview to help the team understand the person's experience of psychosis. The interview also allows the team to meet with the person's family to gather background information that may help with understanding the context of all the symptoms.

Blood tests and other investigations, such as brain scans, may be recommended by the psychiatrist to rule out any physical causes of the symptoms. Neurocognitive testing may also be recommended. This will assess areas such as memory, attention, reasoning, problem solving and speed of processing, which can help highlight cognitive changes resulting from a first episode of psychosis. Neurocognitive testing may provide an indication of the person's potential to recover normal functioning.

Diagnosis and treatment

The information gathered from the assessment will help the team determine the type of psychosis the person is experiencing, its possible causes, and the best way of helping the person. Treatment may be recommended either on an outpatient basis or in hospital. Treatment usually consists of medication and psychosocial interventions (see below).

MEDICATION

Medication is usually essential in the treatment of psychosis. It relieves symptoms of psychosis and plays a critical role in preventing further episodes of illness.

Medications used to treat the symptoms of psychosis are referred to as antipsychotic medications, sometimes known as neuroleptics. These medications are generally divided into two categories: typical (first generation) antipsychotics and the newer atypical (second generation) antipsychotics.

Atypical antipsychotics are increasingly replacing typical antipsychotics as first-line treatments due to the lower risk of extrapyramidal side-effects (see below). These newer antipsychotics differ from one another in terms of their side-effects and, as a result a person may tolerate one medication better than another.

Typical antipsychotic medications have been used for many years, and those that are commonly used include chlorpromazine, flupenthixol, fluphenazine, haloperidol, loxapine, perphenazine, pimozide, thioridazine, thiothixene, trifluoperazine and zuclopenthixol.

The **newer, atypical, antipsychotics** include clozapine (Clozaril), olanzapine (Zyprexa), quetiapine (Seroquel), risperidone (Risperdal), paliperidone (Invega), aripiprazole (Abilify), ziprasidone (Zeldox), lurasidone (Latuda) and asenapine (Saphris).

People with a first psychotic episode tend to respond well to treatment. However, sometimes the person may not continue taking the medication consistently. In these cases a rapid-dissolving or long-acting injectable form of the medication may be used.

Treatment begins with a low dose of medication that is monitored closely for any side-effects. These will usually occur within the first hours, days or weeks of starting treatment. If side-effects develop, the physician may prescribe a lower dose, add a medication to reduce the side-effects, or recommend a different medication altogether.

The details of a specific medication program will be worked out with the physician. If the first antipsychotic medication given does not produce satisfactory results, the patient will usually be given one or two additional trials of the medications listed above. The goal is to use the least amount of medication possible to relieve symptoms, and to keep side-effects to a minimum. Antipsychotic medication may take days or sometimes a few weeks to produce an improvement in psychotic symptoms.

Clozapine is a medication that may prove effective for people who have not responded well to other antipsychotics. It is only used after at least two standard antipsychotics have failed to produce an effective response, because it carries some special risks, including possible harm to white blood cells. While these risks are low, people who take clozapine need to have weekly blood tests to check their white blood cell count.

Antipsychotic medication must be taken even after the symptoms have been relieved. When medication is discontinued too early, there is a very high risk that symptoms will return. This does not necessarily happen right away, and can happen a number of months after medication is stopped. It will be important to talk with your doctor to know how long you should remain on medication.

Side-effects

Many side-effects tend to diminish over time. Some people experience no side-effects.

COMMON SIDE-EFFECTS

Though they are annoying, most side-effects are usually not serious, and diminish over time. They can include fatigue, sedation, dizziness, dry mouth, blurry vision and constipation.

EXTRAPYRAMIDAL SIDE-EFFECTS

This term describes side-effects of restlessness, stiffness, tremor and abnormal involuntary movements.

Extrapyramidal effects include tardive dyskinesia (TD), which refers to involuntary, spontaneous movements of the tongue, lips, jaw or fingers. ("Tardive" means late and "dyskinesia" refers to the kinds of movements that occur.) For every year that a person receives the older, typical antipsychotic medication, there is a five per cent chance of developing tardive dyskinesia. This rate adds up over the years of treatment so that after two years the risk is 10 per cent and after five years it is about 25 per cent. It is believed that this rate is lower for atypical antipsychotics.

If TD does develop, there are ways to identify it at an early stage and to modify treatment. This will reduce the risk that the condition will persist or intensify.

METABOLIC SIDE-EFFECTS
While all antipsychotics can increase body weight, atypical medications as a group are more likely to cause side-effects such as weight gain, high blood levels of glucose and cholesterol, and diabetes. In general, clozapine and olanzapine have the greatest metabolic risk, followed by risperidone and quetiapine. Aripiprazole, ziprasidone, lurasidone, and asenapine are thought to have a lower risk.

These metabolic side-effects can be minimized by lifestyle measures such as proper nutrition and regular exercise.

HORMONAL AND SEXUAL SIDE-EFFECTS
Some antipsychotics can cause changes in sex drive, along with other sexual problems, menstrual changes, and the abnormal production of breast milk (in both sexes).

OTHER MEDICATIONS

Other medications may also be used in conjunction with antipsychotics in treating a first episode of psychosis:
- Benzodiazepines (sedatives) may be used to control agitation while treatment with an antipsychotic is begun at a low dose.
- Antidepressants may be used to treat co-occurring issues such as anxiety and depression.

PSYCHOSOCIAL INTERVENTIONS

Case management

People recovering from a first episode of psychosis often benefit from the services of a case manager or therapist. A case manager co-ordinates the care that the person may need at this time. This person will be a nurse, occupational therapist, psychologist or social worker who has specialized training and experience in psychiatry. A case manager can provide emotional support to the person and the family. Going through a first episode of psychosis may leave you feeling very frightened, confused and overwhelmed. Meeting with and talking to your case manager on a regular basis can help you cope with some of these feelings, and is an important part of recovery.

A case manager can also provide education about the illness and its management, and practical assistance with day-to-day living. This can help the person re-establish a routine, return to work or school, find suitable housing and obtain financial assistance. Case managers may suggest consultation with other team members for specific concerns. They may also recommend programs in the community that contribute to recovery and provide a stepping stone to longer-term goals involving work or school.

A case manager, or another member of the team with specialized expertise, may provide the following interventions, either individually or in group format. Groups are an excellent way to help the young person who has experienced a first episode of psychosis to begin to socialize again with others. Groups can also help a young person feel less alone in their experience.

Psychoeducation

Psychoeducation provides information about the illness, including symptoms, causes and how to manage symptoms and the side-effects of medication. It also includes information on the recovery process, maintaining a sense of well-being, and learning how to prevent a recurrence of the psychosis. Psychoeducation helps the person develop skills such as stress management, problem solving and other life skills.

Vocational and educational counselling

Work and school may often be disrupted for people experiencing a first episode of psychosis. They may worry about their ability to pursue work or school, or need help with career options. If this is the case, a referral to an occupational therapist for short term counselling can help. Occupational therapy explores objectives and interests. Skill-oriented evaluations are used to identify people's strengths and challenges in a work or school setting.

In addition, the case manager can connect the person to resources to help them find employment.

Finally, a referral to a psychologist for neurocognitive testing may be beneficial. This type of assessment evaluates a person's cognitive strengths or limitations. This information can help the person to choose a vocational or educational path that is suited to them, and identify any potential accommodations that may help them to succeed.

Cognitive-behavioural therapy

Cognitive-behavioural therapy (CBT) explores the connection between thoughts, feelings and behaviours. The way a person thinks can affect how they feel and behave. CBT can help a person to develop healthier ways of thinking, which can lead to a change in feelings and behaviour. CBT has been shown to help those recovering from psychosis to work on issues such as understanding the impact of the illness, coping more effectively with stress, and recognizing the impact of alcohol and other drugs on symptoms.

CBT can also help with finding alternative, healthy ways to cope with illness, reducing symptoms, and preventing relapse. CBT may be offered in a group format or individually.

Dialectical behaviour therapy

Dialectical behaviour therapy (DBT) helps a person manage overwhelming emotions, and strengthens their ability to effectively manage distressing situations. It may include individual sessions as well as group therapy. Skills that are taught include coping effectively with distressing situations, focusing on the present moment, avoiding getting overwhelmed by emotions, and developing effective interpersonal skills.

Cognitive-behavioural social skills training

Cognitive-behavioural social skills training (CBSST) combines CBT and social skills training techniques to help people achieve their social, behavioural or vocational goals. This approach helps people to catch, check and change unhelpful thoughts that may be interfering with achieving their goals. It also teaches communication and problem-solving skills.

Motivational interviewing

It can be difficult for anyone to make changes in their life. People often have mixed feelings, or ambivalence, about change. Motivational interviewing (MI) is an approach to helping people who are thinking about making a change. It is a collaborative process that can help people explore their motivation and ambivalence about making the change, and strengthen their commitment to the change.

Acceptance and commitment therapy

Acceptance and commitment therapy (ACT) helps a person who may feel stuck on certain thoughts, to notice and accept their thoughts, and to view the thoughts as separate from their sense of self. It also helps the person to focus on the present moment. In this way, ACT helps you develop greater psychological flexibility, enhances your commitment to your key values, and helps you take actions toward doing the things you value.

Mindfulness meditation

Mindfulness is defined as "the awareness that emerges through paying attention on purpose, in the present moment, and non-judgmentally to the unfolding of experience" (Kabat-Zinn, 2003). It is a skill that can be learned, and can be helpful in increasing self-awareness, relaxation and the ability to cope with difficult situations or overwhelming emotions.

Cognitive adaptation training

A person experiencing psychosis can also experience cognitive symptoms, such as difficulty in solving problems, that can make everyday functioning difficult. Cognitive adaptation training (CAT) helps the person to work around their cognitive difficulties to improve their daily functioning, including taking medication and self-care. After a comprehensive assessment is completed, appropriate environmental supports to help functioning (such as signs and checklists) are put into place in the person's living environment.

Treatment for concurrent disorders

Research shows that when a person with psychosis also has substance use problems, it is most effective to treat them together. For this reason, first episode psychosis programs provide treatment for substance use as well as for symptoms of psychosis. The substance use treatment may be within the program or provided by an external agency. It may include assessment; group and/or individual counselling; and education about substances, the impact on symptoms of psychosis, medication management, stress management and relapse prevention.

7 Family involvement—issues and concerns

Many partners and families find the onset of psychosis extremely distressing and feel helpless and confused. Family involvement is important in the overall plan toward recovery. Family members can be an important part of the treatment team. They can provide information about the person's symptoms, how they developed, and how the person functioned before the onset of psychosis, which can be very helpful information for the treatment team. It is also important that family members take care of themselves, and if necessary get help with their own concerns and distress.

Family members can learn about the nature of the illness, and available treatment options available for their family member, by working with the treatment team. Family members can also receive guidance on issues such as how to relate to, and support, a relative who is ill. For example, it is best to communicate in a calm, clear manner, and to avoid overwhelming the person with too much information. It is also important for family members to be aware that their relatives need time to recover and may not be able to fully engage in all activities of daily living right away. A structured approach to gradually taking on tasks and activities usually works best.

Many families find that they need to develop coping strategies and effective communication skills to help them support the family member experiencing psychosis. Individual family counselling, psychoeducation workshops and support groups can help develop these strategies and skills.

These groups and workshops can also provide the families themselves with emotional and practical support, as well as education about the illness. It is important that family members find a balance between supporting their recovering relative and finding time for themselves. This helps them prevent exhaustion and avoid becoming "burned out."

The CAMH book *Promoting Recovery from First Episode Psychosis: A Guide for Families* is another valuable resource for families.

8 The process of recovery

People dealing with a first episode of psychosis should be actively involved in their own treatment and recovery. This can be achieved by learning about the illness and its treatment, and the ways to prevent further episodes. The recovery process will be more successful if the person learns to recognize warning signs or symptoms, learns how to manage stress, builds up a social support network, and engages in valued activities, such as work, school or leisure.

A final word about recovery

The course of recovery from a first episode of psychosis varies from person to person. Sometimes symptoms go away quickly and people are able to resume a normal life right away. For others, it may take several weeks or months to recover, and they may need support over a longer period of time.

Remember: psychosis is treatable and many people will make an excellent recovery.

References

Brabban, A. & Turkington, D. (2002). The search for meaning: Detecting congruence between life events, underlying schema and psychotic symptoms. In A. P. Morrison (Ed.), *A Casebook of Cognitive Therapy for Psychosis*. Hove, England: Brunner-Routledge.

Kabat-Zinn, J. (2003). Mindfulness-based interventions in context: Past, present, and future. *Clinical Psychology: Science and Practice*, *10* (2), 144–156.

Resources

Martens, L. & Baker, S. (2009). *Promoting Recovery from First Episode Psychosis: A Guide for Families.* Toronto: CAMH.

BC Early Psychosis Intervention Program: www.psychosissucks.ca

Canadian Mental Health Association: www.cmha.ca

Centre for Addiction and Mental Health (CAMH): www.camh.ca

Ontario Working Group for Early Psychosis Intervention: www.epion.ca

Psychosis 101: www.psychosis101.ca

Other guides in this series

Addiction

Anxiety Disorders

Bipolar Disorder

Borderline Personality Disorder

Cognitive-Behavioural Therapy

Concurrent Substance Use and Mental Health Disorders

Depression

Dual Diagnosis

First Episode Psychosis

The Forensic Mental Health System in Ontario

Obsessive-Compulsive Disorder

Schizophrenia

Women, Abuse and Trauma Therapy

Women and Psychosis

To order these and other CAMH publications,
contact Sales and Distribution:
Toll-free: 1 800 661-1111
Toronto: 416 595-6059
E-mail: publications@camh.ca
Online store: http://store.camh.ca